Audio Access Included - Recorded Accompaniments Online

THE DEVELOPING CLASSICAL SINGER - TENOR

Songs by British and American Composers

THE DEVELOPING
Classical
Singer

TENOR

ISBN 978-1-4950-9433-0

To access companion recorded piano accompaniments online, visit:
www.halleonard.com/mylibrary

Enter Code
2649-4012-9772-7033

BOOSEY & HAWKES

AN IMAGEM COMPANY

DISTRIBUTED BY

HAL•LEONARD®
7777 W. BLUEMOUND RD. P.O. BOX 13819 MILWAUKEE, WI 53213

www.boosey.com
www.halleonard.com

PREFACE

The Developing Classical Singer was compiled from the rich choices in the Boosey & Hawkes catalogue, with songs in English by British and American composers. The selection of songs is for the teenage voice, or an early level collegiate singer, or an adult amateur taking voice lessons.

The songs were chosen with some specific issues in mind: vocal ranges that are not extreme, and musical challenges that are manageable for a singer at this level. Beyond art song, we have included folksong arrangements, such as those by Aaron Copland and Benjamin Britten, which are fully composed in the spirit of an art song, designed for a classical voice.

There are different compilations for each voice type: soprano, mezzo-soprano, tenor and baritone. Some cornerstone songs are in all volumes, because of their beauty and appropriateness for any voice. These include Britten's "O Waly, Waly"; Ireland's "Spring Sorrow"; Britten's realization of Purcell's "I attempt from love's sickness to fly"; Quilter's "Weep you no more"; and Vaughan Williams' "Bright is the ring of words." Beyond that, it is the editor's subjective choice about which songs work best for each voice type. Gender is certainly a factor in this, but also just the vocal sound and color of a song. Original keys of the songs were considered, but since nearly every composer of art song is not opposed to transposition, original keys were not a confining factor in which volume a song lands.

A few pedagogical reasons for assigning songs to students, though many other topics could be addressed:

Agility
I attempt from love's sickness to fly
I'll sail upon the Dog-star
The Nightingale

Breath Support for a Long Phrase
Oh fair to see
The Salley Gardens

Building an Expressive Legato Phrase
As Ever I Saw
How love came in
Fairest Isle
Long Time Ago
O Waly, Waly
Since we loved
Spring Sorrow
Weep you no more

Expanding Vocal Range
I'll sail upon the Dog-star
O mistress mine

Dynamic Contrasts
The Boatmen's Dance

Sensitively Expressing Poetry
Bright is the ring of words
Little Elegy
Spring Sorrow
Stopping by Woods on a Snowy Evening
Take, O take those lips away

Personality and Storytelling
Barbara Allen
I bought me a cat
Linden Lea
Master Kilby
Money, O!
The Vagabond

Tenor voices come in many varieties. Many young tenors have faint sound in the low notes, and with that in mind, notes below the E below middle C appear infrequently in these songs in these keys. There are songs for those voices more comfortable staying below F above middle C. And there are some songs for those voices that naturally and easily sing higher in the range. However, the highest vocal note in this entire book is the G above middle C, which keeps it to a student singer's range.

Beyond the music, singers should learn to consider the words carefully, understanding them apart from the music, and pondering what the composer intended with the setting of the words to notes. This is the way into true personal expression, and is the real secret to becoming an artist as a performer of art song.

Richard Walters
Editor

CONTENTS

Pianists on the recordings: [1] Laura Ward, [2] Brendan Fox, [3] Richard Walters

How love came in
original key

ROBERT HERRICK

LENNOX BERKELEY

WINTHROP ROGERS EDITION

but I as well as an-y oth-er this____ can tell; That when from hence____ she does de- part, The out-let then____ ____ is from the heart.____

Master Kilby

from *Folksong Arrangements Volume 6: England*

original key: a major 2nd higher

*Words and Melody from
"Folk Songs for Schools"
collected and arranged by CECIL J. SHARP

Folk Song from Somerset
Arranged for voice and guitar by
BENJAMIN BRITTEN
Transcribed for piano by
Richard Walters

1. In the heat of the
2. Then I pull'd off my

day When the sun shines so free - ly, There I met Mas - ter
hat And I bowed to the ground ___ And I said: "Mas - ter

Kil - by, ___ So ___ fine and so gay.
Kil - by, ___ Pray ___ where are you bound?"

O Waly, Waly

from Somerset (Cecil Sharp)*

from *Folksong Arrangements Volume 3: British Isles*

original key

Arranged by
BENJAMIN BRITTEN

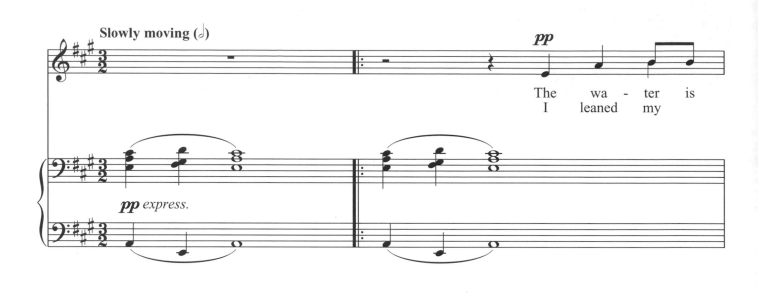

The wa - ter is
I leaned my

wide I can - not get o'er, and nei - ther have I wings to
back up a - gainst some oak think - ing that he was a trust - y

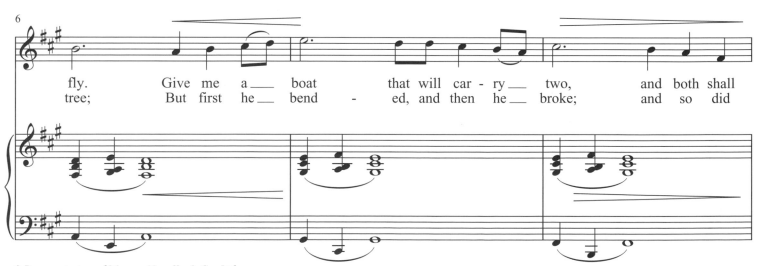

fly. Give me a boat that will car - ry two, and both shall
tree; But first he bend - ed, and then he broke; and so did

* By permission of Messrs. Novello & Co. Ltd.

O, love is hand - some and love is fine, and love's a

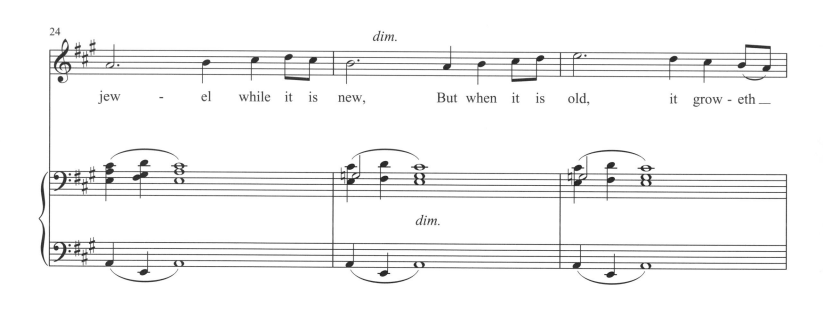

jew - el while it is new, But when it is old, it grow - eth

cold, and fades a - way like morn - ing dew.

To Clytie Mundy

The Salley Gardens

Irish Tune

from *Folksong Arrangements Volume 1: British Isles*

original key: a minor 2nd higher

*Words by
W. B. YEATS

Arranged by
BENJAMIN BRITTEN

*The words of this song are reprinted from "Collected Poems of W. B. Yeats" by permission of Mrs. Yeats.

The Boatmen's Dance

(Minstrel Song-1843)

from *Old American Songs, First Set*

original key: a minor 2nd lower

Arranged by
AARON COPLAND

2nd time

As at first (♪ = 63)

f *legato*

High row the boat-men row float-in' down the riv - er the O - hi - o.____

Fast tempo (♩ = 126)

mf

3. The boat - man is a thrift - y man There's none can do as the

boat - man can I nev - er see a pret - ty gal in my life But

that she was a boat - man's wife O dance the boat-men dance, O

stacc.

(mark the bass)

I bought me a cat

(Children's Song)

from *Old American Songs, First Set*

original key: a minor 3rd lower

Arranged by
AARON COPLAND

hen says "Shim - my shack, shim - my shack" My goose says "Quaw, quaw" My

duck says "Quaa, quaa" My cat says fid - dle eye fee. I

bought me a horse My horse pleased me I fed my horse un - der

yon - der tree My horse says "Neigh, neigh" My cow says "Baw, baw" My

Long Time Ago
(Ballad)

from *Old American Songs, First Set*

original key: a major 2nd lower

Arranged by
AARON COPLAND

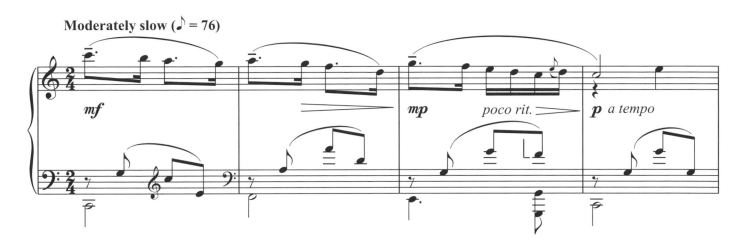

Bird and bee and blos - som taught her Love's___ spell___ to know_____

— While to my fond words she lis-ten'd Mur - mur - ing___

low Ten - der - ly her blue eyes glis-ten'd

Long time_ a - go._____

Oh fair to see

from *Oh fair to see*
original key

CHRISTINA ROSSETTI

GERALD FINZI
Op. 13b, No. 2

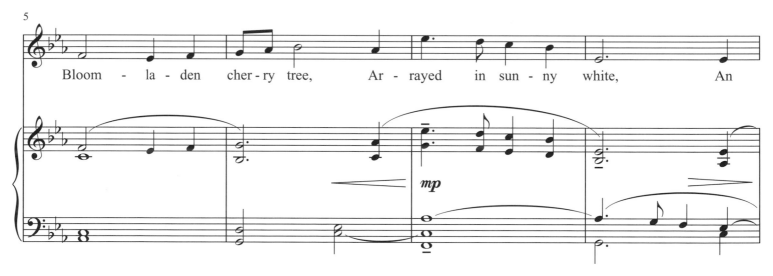

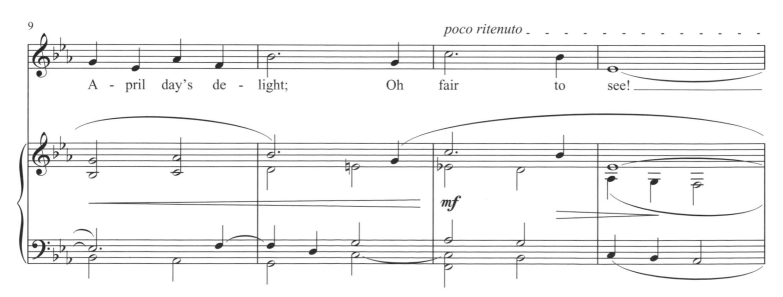

1929
[1' 5]

Since we loved

from *Oh fair to see*

original key: a major 2nd higher

ROBERT BRIDGES *

GERALD FINZI
Op. 13b, No. 7

Since we loved,—— (the earth that shook as we kissed,

fresh beau-ty took)—— Love hath been as po-ets

paint, Life as heav-en is to a saint;

† This is Gerald Finzi's last song. It was completed a month before he died.

* Poem reprinted by kind permission of The Clarendon Press, Oxford.

August 28, 1956
[1' 0]

To Hester Berry

Money, O!

from *Songs of the Countryside*

original key: a major 2nd lower

W.H. DAVIES

MICHAEL HEAD

down. _____ When I had mon-ey, _____ mon-ey, O! _____ I knew no joy till I went poor For man-y a false man as a friend Came knock-ing all day at my door, all day at my door. _____

Headley Down, Sept. 1928

Spring Sorrow

original key: a minor 3rd lower

RUPERT BROOKE   JOHN IRELAND

This Poem is reprinted from "1914 and other Poems" by Rupert Brooke,
by permission of the Literary Executor and Messrs Sidgwick and Jackson Ltd.

pain. My __ heart all Win - ter lay so numb, The

earth so dead and frore, That I nev - er thought __ the

Spring would come, Or my heart wake an - y more. But

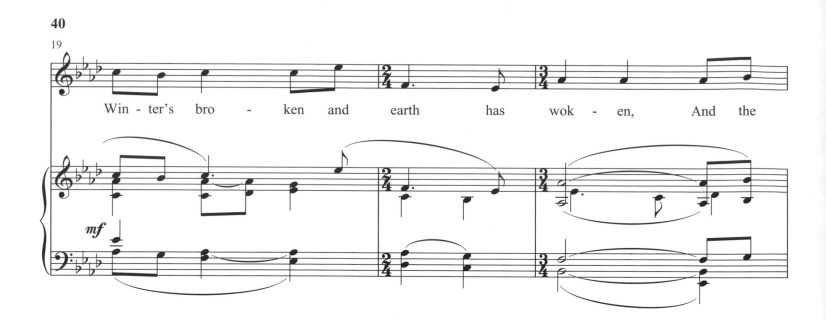

Win - ter's bro - ken and earth has wok - en, And the

small birds cry a - gain; And the haw-thorn hedge _ puts forth its buds And my

heart puts forth its pain. _____

April, 1918

Fairest Isle

from *Seven Songs* (Orpheus Britannicus)
original key: a minor 3rd higher

JOHN DRYDEN

HENRY PURCELL
realized by
BENJAMIN BRITTEN

I'll sail upon the Dog-star

from *Seven Songs* (Orpheus Britannicus)

original key

THOMAS D'URFEY

HENRY PURCELL
realized by
BENJAMIN BRITTEN

I attempt from love's sickness to fly

from *Five Songs* (Orpheus Britannicus)

original key: a major 2nd higher

JOHN DRYDEN
and ROBERT HOWARD

HENRY PURCELL
realized by
BENJAMIN BRITTEN

To the memory of Arnold Guy Vivian

Barbara Allen
from *The Arnold Book of Old Songs*
original key: a minor 3rd lower

TRADITIONAL

Old English Melody
arranged by
ROGER QUILTER

month of May When green buds they were swel - lin', Young

Jem - my Grove on his death - bed lay For love of Bar - b'ra

Al - len.

Then slow - ly, slow - ly she came up, And

knel - lin', And ev - 'ry stroke the __ dead - bell gave Cried

"Woe to Bar - b'ra Al- len!"

When he was dead and laid in grave Her

heart was struck with sor - row, "O moth- er, moth - er, __ make my bed, For

To Walter Creighton

O mistress mine

from *Three Shakespeare Songs, First Set*

original key: a major 3rd lower

WILLIAM SHAKESPEARE
from *Twelfth Night*

ROGER QUILTER
Op. 6, No. 2

To the memory of my friend, Mrs. Cary-Elwes

Weep you no more

from *Seven Elizabethan Lyrics*

original key: a minor 2nd higher

ANONYMOUS

ROGER QUILTER
Op. 12, No. 1

To A.C. Landsberg

Take, O take those lips away

from *Five Shakespeare Songs, Second Set*

WILLIAM SHAKESPEARE
from *Measure for Measure*

original key: a major 3rd lower

ROGER QUILTER
Op. 23, No. 4

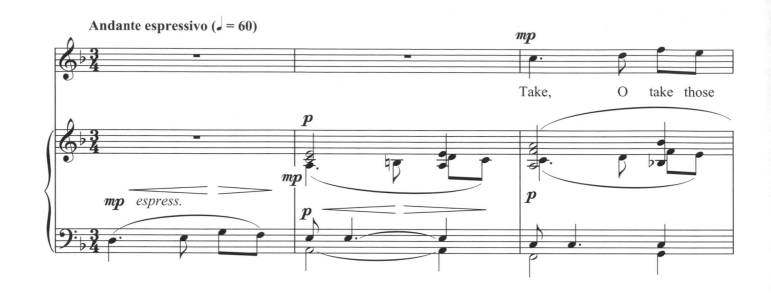

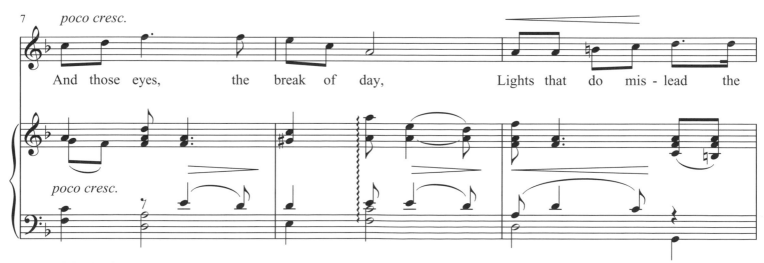

To Muriel Smith

The Nightingale

original key

NED ROREM

About 1500 A.D.

Fast and delicate and supple ($\quad$ = 112 or more)

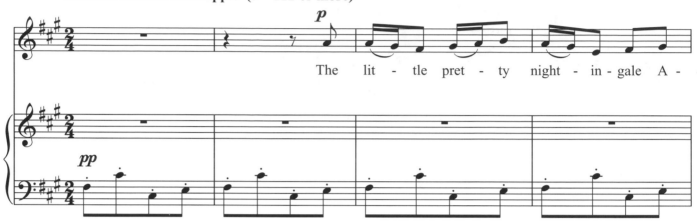

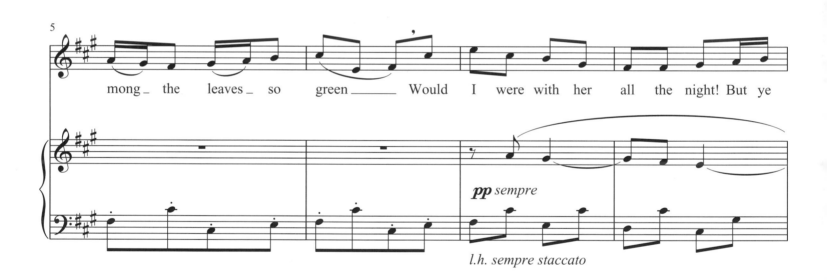

Marrakech, 11 August 1951

To Nell Tangeman
Little Elegy
original key

ELINOR WYLIE

NED ROREM

New York City, 28 March 1948
(Spring, cool, bright, noon)

for my father
Stopping by Woods on a Snowy Evening
original key

ROBERT FROST

NED ROREM

on - ly oth - er sound's the sweep Of eas - y wind and down - y flake.

The woods are love - ly, dark and deep. But I have prom - is - es to keep, And

miles to go be - fore I sleep, And miles to go be - fore I

sleep.

New York City, Thursday, 20 March 1947

As Ever I Saw

original key

ANONYMOUS

PETER WARLOCK

see ___ her dance! ___ She will the best ___ her-
self ___ ad - vance, That ev - er I saw. To
see her fin - gers that be ___ so small! In my con - ceit ___ she
pass - eth all that ev - er I saw.

Na - ture in her hath won - der - ly wrought Christ nev - er such an -

oth - er bought, That ev - er I saw.

I have seen man - y that __ have beau - ty Yet is there none __

like to my la - dy that ev - er I saw.

Therefore I dare this boldly say I shall have the best and fairest may That ever I saw, that ever I saw.

To Mrs. Edmund Fisher

Linden Lea
A Dorset Song

original key: a major 2nd lower

WILLIAM BARNES

RALPH VAUGHAN WILLIAMS

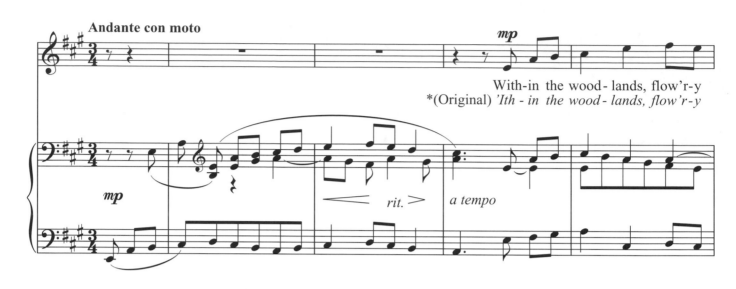

With-in the wood-lands, flow'r-y
*(Original) 'Ith - in the wood-lands, flow'r-y

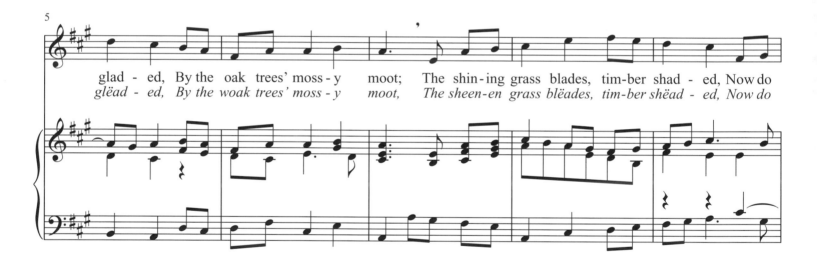

glad - ed, By the oak trees' moss-y moot; The shin-ing grass blades, tim-ber shad - ed, Now do
glëad - ed, By the woak trees' moss-y moot, The sheen-en grass blëades, tim-ber shëad - ed, Now do

quiv-er un-der foot; And birds do whis-tle o-ver-head, And wa-ter's bub-bling in its
quiv-er un-der voot; An' birds do whis-sle au-ver-head, An' wa-ter's bub-blen in its

*The original text by William Barnes is in Dorset dialect.
Dorset dialect was spoken in Dorset county in southwestern England.

bed;   And there for me,   The ap-ple tree Do lean down low in Lin - den Lea
bed;   An' there vor me,   The ap-ple tree Do lean down low in Lin - den Lea.

When leaves, that late - ly   were a - spring - ing, Now do
When leaves, that lëate - ly   were a - spring - en, Now do

fade with - in the copse,   And paint-ed birds do hush their sing - ing, Up up-
fade 'ith - in the copse,   An' paint-ed birds do hush their zing - en, Up up-

on the tim - ber tops; And brown leaved fruit's a - turn - ing red, In cloud-less
on the tim - ber tops; An' brown leaved fruit's a - turn - ing red, In cloud-less

sun - shine o - ver-head, With fruit for me, the ap-ple tree Do lean down low in Lin - den
zun - sheen au-ver-head, Wi' fruit vor me, the ap-ple tree Do lean down low in Lin - den

colla voce

Animato *f*

Lea.
Lea.

mp

rit.

a tempo
f

Let oth - er folk make mo-ney
Let oth - er vo'k meäke mo-ney

fas - ter; In the air of dark - room'd towns; I don't dread a peev - ish
vas - ter, In the air o' dark - room'd towns; I don't dread a peev - ish

master, Though no man may heed my frowns. I be free to go a-
meäs - ter, Though noo man may heed my frowns. I be free to go a-

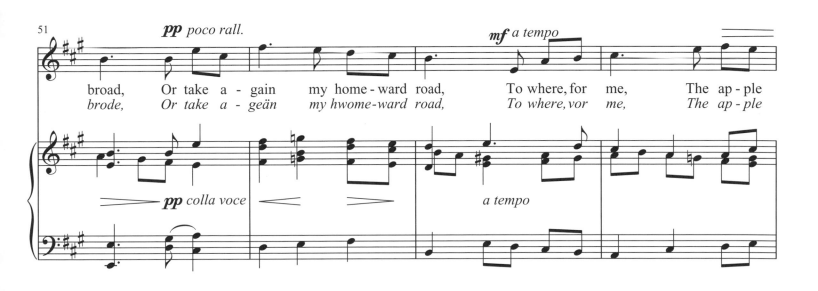

broad, Or take a - gain my home - ward road, To where, for me, The ap - ple
brode, Or take a - geän my hwome-ward road, To where, vor me, The ap - ple

tree Do lean down low in Lin - den Lea.
tree Do lean down low in Lin - den Lea.

The Vagabond

from *Songs of Travel*

original key: a major 3rd lower

ROBERT LOUIS STEVENSON

RALPH VAUGHAN WILLIAMS

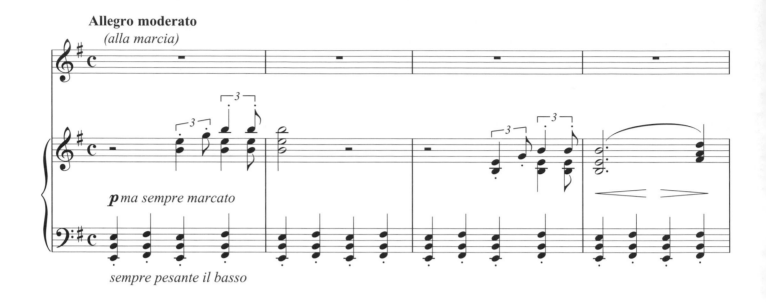

Bed in the bush with stars to see, Bread I dip in the ri -

ver— There's the life for a man like me, _____ There's the

life for ev - er.

colla voce

Let the blow fall soon or late, Let what will be

o'er me; Give the face of earth a - round, And the road be - fore me.

Wealth I seek not, hope nor love, Nor a ___ friend to know

me; All I seek, the heaven a - bove, ___ And the

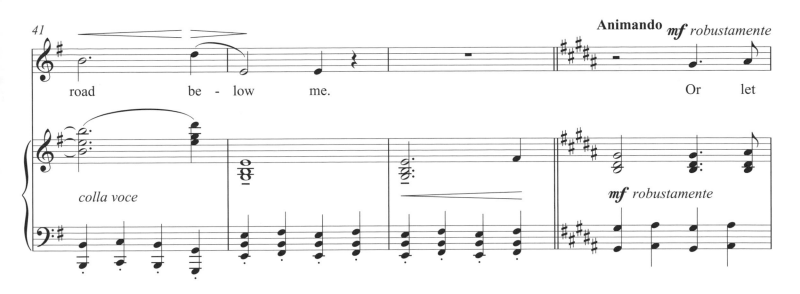

White as meal the fros - ty field— Warm the fire - side ha - ven—

Not to au - tumn will I yield, Not to win - ter e - ven!

Let the blow fall soon or late, Let what will be o'er me; Give the face of earth a-

round, And the road be-fore me. Wealth I ask not, hope nor love,

Nor a___ friend to know me; All I ask, the heaven a-

bove,___ And the road be - low me.

Bright is the ring of words

from *Songs of Travel*

original key: a perfect 4th lower

ROBERT LOUIS STEVENSON

RALPH VAUGHAN WILLIAMS